EDGE
BOOKS

BUG WARS

PRAYING MANTIS VS. GIANT HORNET

BY ALICIA Z. KLEPEIS

BATTLE OF THE POWERFUL PREDATORS

CONSULTANT:
Christiane Weirauch
Professor of Entomology,
Department of Entomology
University of California, Riverside

CAPSTONE PRESS
a capstone imprint

Edge Books are published by Capstone Press,
1710 Roe Crest Drive, North Mankato, Minnesota 56003
www.mycapstone.com

Library of Congress Cataloging-in-Publication Data
Klepeis, Alicia, 1971- author.
Praying mantis vs. Giant hornet : battle of the powerful predators / by Alicia Z. Klepeis.
    pages cm.—(Edge. Bug wars)
  Audience: Ages 9-10.
  Audience: Grades 4 to 6.
ISBN 978-1-4914-8067-0 (library binding)
ISBN 978-1-4914-8071-7 (pbk.)
1. Praying mantis—Juvenile literature. 2. Hornets—Juvenile literature. 3. Predatory
animals—Juvenile literature. I. Title. II. Title: Praying mantis versus Giant hornet.
  QL505.9.M35K54 2016
  595—dc23
                    2015024331

Editorial Credits
Nate LeBoutillier, editor; Russell Griesmer, designer; Katy LaVigne, production specialist

Photo Credits
Getty Images: Digital Vision, 13 (left), 25, 27; James P. Rowan, 29; Minden Pictures:
FLPA/S & D & K Maslowski, Cover (left), Cover (back), 5, Nature Production/Satoshi
Kuribayashi, Cover (right), 4, 6, 9 (top), 11 (top), 21 (top); Newscom: Minden Pictures/
Michael Durham, 11 (bottom); Science Source: Lawrence Lawry, 17, Scott Camazine,
24; Shutterstock: Cristian Gusa, 13 (right), Cristian Gusa, 19 (bottom), Cristian Gusa,
22, Evgeniy Ayupov, 9 (bottom), 23, pattara puttiwong, 7, POPUMON, 15, Stubblefield
Photography, 19 (top); UIG via Getty Images/Education Images, 21 (bottom)

Design Elements
Capstone and Shutterstock:

Printed and bound in US.
007521CGS16

TABLE OF CONTENTS

WELCOME TO BUG WARS!

A bug is often a savage creature. It searches for **prey**, finds it, and goes in for the kill. Sometimes one bug can easily overpower its victim. A crafty spider might catch an unsuspecting fly in its web. A single Asian giant hornet has been known to kill 40 honeybees per minute. That's one corpse every 1.5 seconds! But in Bug Wars, there's no clear winner. Carnivores attack other **carnivores**. Giant bugs take on other huge insects. All kinds of bug battles are possible!

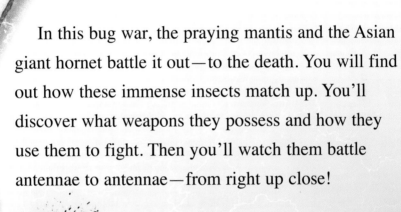

In this bug war, the praying mantis and the Asian giant hornet battle it out—to the death. You will find out how these immense insects match up. You'll discover what weapons they possess and how they use them to fight. Then you'll watch them battle antennae to antennae—from right up close!

FIERCE FACT

AFRICA'S KALAHARI BUSHMEN BELIEVE THE MANTIS IS SACRED AND THAT IT REPRESENTS THE GOD OF CREATION.

prey—an animal hunted by another animal for food

carnivore—an animal that eats meat

THE COMBATANTS

The Chinese mantis is one species of about 2,400 different species of praying mantises worldwide. It may not actually fight very often with the Asian giant hornet. But both terrifying insects live in China, Japan, and other parts of Asia. They are some of the largest bugs in all of Asia. Each of these fierce insects can cause an enemy serious pain.

The Chinese mantis crunches all kinds of critters. It makes meals of bugs, lizards and even hummingbirds.

Asian giant hornets often destroy their fellow insects quite easily. They sometimes hunt in groups. Just 30 Asian giant hornets can completely wipe out a colony housing 10,000 European honeybees in an hour. Talk about a massacre!

These two predators might not bother to hunt each other much. After all, they could easily prey on smaller insects. But you never know—these hungry bugs look for food anywhere they can find it!

CHINESE MANTIDS CAME TO THE
UNITED STATES IN THE LATE 1800S.
THEY WERE, PERHAPS, STOWAWAYS ON
A BOAT THAT WAS SHIPPING PLANTS.
TODAY THE CHINESE MANTIS IS THE
LARGEST AND MOST COMMONLY SEEN
MANTIS IN THE UNITED STATES.

species—a group of animals with similar features

predator—an animal that hunts other animals for food

SIZE

The Chinese mantis is a large, strong predator. It measures up to 5 inches (12.7 centimeters) long. That's about as long as a smartphone. Its wingspan averages about 3 to 4 inches (8 to 10 cm) long. Despite its large size, the Chinese mantis is a lightweight. At around 0.11 ounces (3 grams), it's as heavy as a penny. The Chinese mantis' size and strength could overpower most insect enemies.

The Asian giant hornet is the world's largest hornet species. Worker and drone Asian hornets measure about 1.4 inches (3.6 cm) long. That's roughly the size of a child's thumb. The queen's body is bigger at more than 2 inches (5 cm) long. This hornet's wingspan could spread the width of your hand at roughly 3 inches (8 cm) wide. The Asian giant hornet weighs 20 times as much as a honeybee. Although it's smaller than the Chinese mantis, the giant hornet's size makes it tough to defeat in a fight.

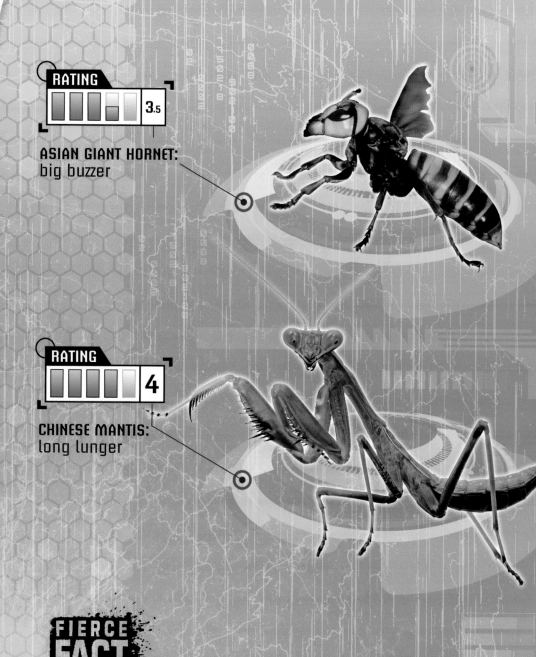

RATING

3.5

ASIAN GIANT HORNET:
big buzzer

RATING

4

CHINESE MANTIS:
long lunger

FIERCE FACT

IN JAPAN, ASIAN GIANT HORNETS ARE REFERRED TO AS
"SPARROW WASPS" BECAUSE THEY ARE SO LARGE THAT
THEY RESEMBLE SMALL BIRDS.

SPEED AND AGILITY

The Chinese mantis takes its time—until it's ready to strike. Its average walking speed is slower than a three-toed sloth's. Mantids usually only fly to escape a predator or to get to a new perch. Their slow cruising speed while in flight is only about half as fast as the bats which hunt them.

But when snaring prey, the Chinese mantis moves super fast. A mantis strike has been measured at 30 to 50 one-thousandths of a second. How fast is this? A mantis could strike twice in the time it takes to blink your eye!

Asian giant hornets aren't fast on their feet. They usually only walk when they're building their ground-level nests.

The Asian giant hornet is a much faster flyer than its mantis enemy. It can cruise the skies at 25 miles (40 kilometers) per hour. That's speedier than most adults can bike down a steep hill. This flight speed is a real advantage when tracking down prey. They can cover 50 to 60 miles (80 to 95 km) a day while flying.

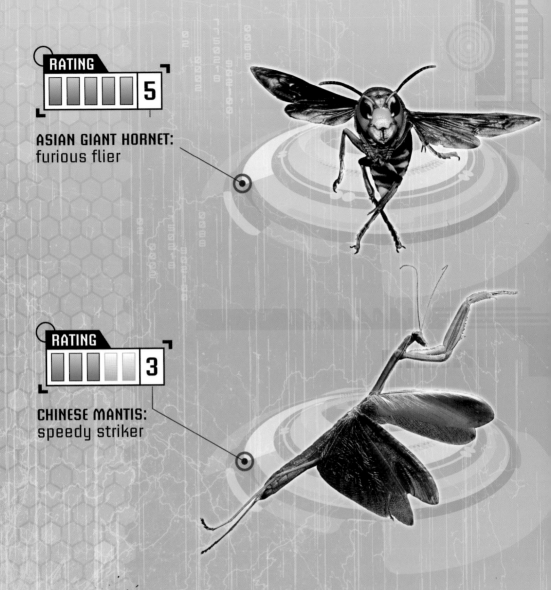

RATING

☐☐☐☐☐ **5**

ASIAN GIANT HORNET:
furious flier

RATING

☐☐☐☐☐ **3**

CHINESE MANTIS:
speedy striker

FIERCE FACT

ASIAN GIANT HORNETS WILL CHASE HUMANS. THEY
ARE VERY ATTRACTED TO HUMAN SWEAT, FAST
MOVEMENTS, AND SWEET SMELLS.

DEFENSES

The Chinese mantis has a tough **exoskeleton**. This protects its guts if attacked. The mantis' bulging **compound eyes** give it excellent vision. They allow it to see in several directions at once. They also help judge distances very accurately—up to 65 feet (20 meters) away, an amazing distance for an insect.

The Chinese mantis has great **camouflage** to keep it hidden from predators and prey. Its pale green or tan hue blends in with the plants it lives on. Its long, skinny body resembles a twig that sways. Even its wings look like thin leaves.

Just like its enemy, the Asian giant hornet has antennae that gather sensory information. The hornet can also see in multiple directions at once.

Unlike the Chinese mantis, the Asian giant hornet doesn't blend into the background. Instead, its bright yellow-orange coloring serves a protective purpose. It tells potential predators, "Stay away—I'm **toxic**!"

The Asian giant hornet can stay out of sight. Its nests are often built underground or in tree hollows. But if it buzzes out, other bugs should beware!

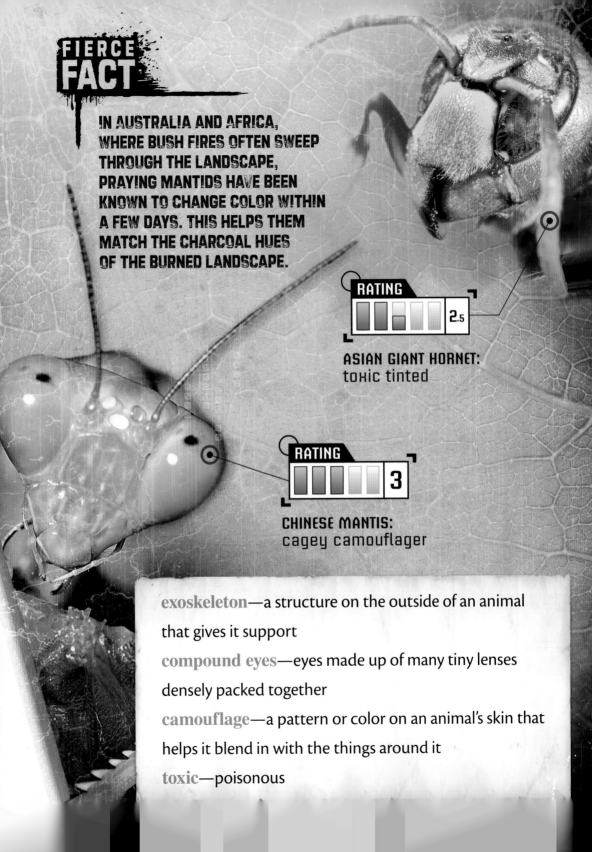

FIERCE FACT

IN AUSTRALIA AND AFRICA, WHERE BUSH FIRES OFTEN SWEEP THROUGH THE LANDSCAPE, PRAYING MANTIDS HAVE BEEN KNOWN TO CHANGE COLOR WITHIN A FEW DAYS. THIS HELPS THEM MATCH THE CHARCOAL HUES OF THE BURNED LANDSCAPE.

RATING 2.5

ASIAN GIANT HORNET:
toxic tinted

RATING 3

CHINESE MANTIS:
cagey camouflager

PRAYING MANTIS WEAPONS

The Chinese mantis has strong, folded forelegs. These can spring into action at lightning speed. Mantids can even snatch flying insects right out of the air. Its forelegs feature an array of hooks and spines arranged to serve as a trap.

After catching its prey, the Chinese mantis may even nibble strips of flesh away while its prey is still alive. They can decapitate an enemy faster than you can say "Look out!"

FIERCE FACT

AT ONLY 1-2 INCHES (3-5 CM) LONG, THE SPINY FLOWER MANTIS IS ONE OF THE SMALLER MANTIDS. DESPITE ITS SMALL SIZE, THIS BRIGHTLY COLORED BUG IS A LIGHTNING-FAST PREDATOR WITH FIRST-RATE HUNTING SKILLS.

RATING

☐☐☐☐☐ 3

CHINESE MANTIS:
champion chewer

foreleg—a front leg

decapitate—to cut off the head

15

GIANT HORNET WEAPONS

The Asian giant hornet's stinger packs a serious punch. It's only about the length of an eraser on a pencil. But unlike most bees' stingers, this deadly weapon can be used again and again.

The Asian giant hornet's sting is very painful to prey. Its stinger injects fast-acting **venom**, which is deadly. It destroys red blood cells and can dissolve flesh.

Located on the outside of the hornet's mouth are its **mandibles**. These slice through the bodies of prey. The Asian giant hornet's mandibles cut, chew, and tear food apart. They also come in handy when carrying dead victims around.

FIERCE FACT

WHEN PEOPLE ARE STUNG BY ASIAN GIANT HORNETS, THEIR SKIN LOOKS LIKE IT HAS BEEN PIERCED BY BULLET HOLES. ONE VICTIM DESCRIBED HIS GIANT HORNET BITE AS FEELING "LIKE A HOT NAIL THROUGH MY LEG."

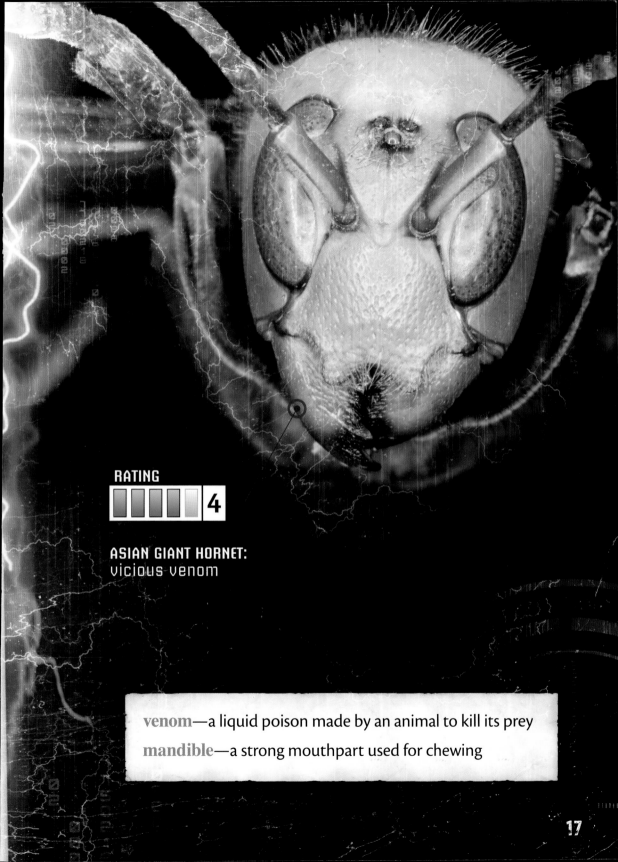

RATING

4

ASIAN GIANT HORNET:
vicious venom

venom—a liquid poison made by an animal to kill its prey

mandible—a strong mouthpart used for chewing

WEAKNESSES

Even with their wicked weapons, the Chinese mantis and Asian giant hornet aren't totally without weaknesses. Both insects try catching prey off-guard. The sit-and-wait hunting style of the mantis can leave him open to attackers. Waiting for his prey, the mantis might become another predator's meal. Even when retreating, mantids travel slowly. Compared to the hasty hornet, this is tortoise-like! And females, which fly only rarely, are at a major disadvantage. The Chinese mantis also has a weak sense of smell. So it may not sniff what's creeping up behind it.

The Asian giant hornet is fast but has trouble hiding. Unlike the mantis, the hornet's yellow-orange color tends to alert enemies. And it only has a stinger at one end of its body. This leaves it vulnerable to an attack from the side or below its abdomen.

FIERCE FACT

AS A LAST RESORT TO ESCAPE A PREDATOR, A MANTIS MAY SACRIFICE ONE OR MORE OF ITS LEGS. A MANTIS WITHOUT FRONT LEGS—WHICH ARE USED FOR HUNTING—USUALLY DIES QUICKLY OF STARVATION.

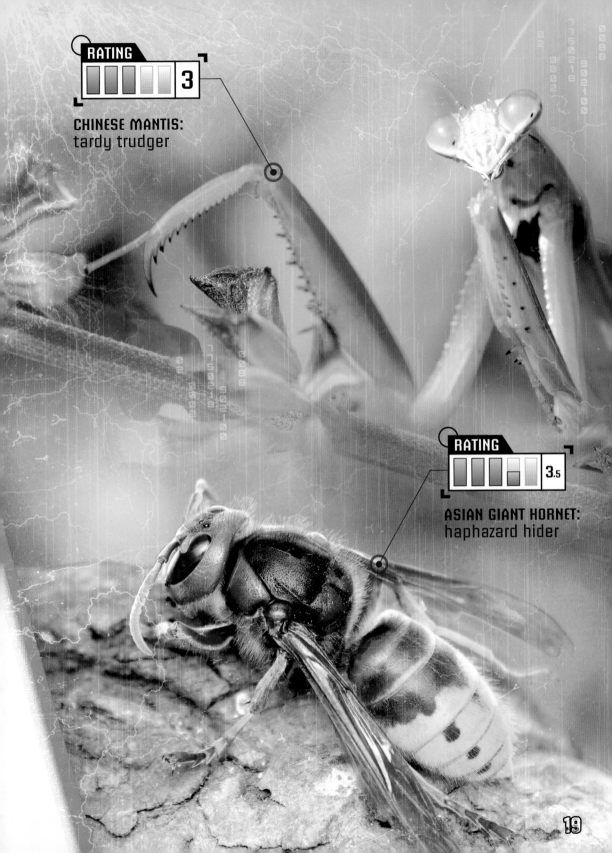

RATING
3

CHINESE MANTIS:
tardy trudger

RATING
3.5

ASIAN GIANT HORNET:
haphazard hider

19

ATTACK STYLE

The Chinese mantis is a crafty hunter. It blends in with the surrounding vegetation until prey gets close enough. Then the mantis lashes out and quickly grabs its victim. Its spiny front legs pierce the prey and act as a trap. The mantis is likely to start by biting its enemy's head off. But it could also chew through almost any other body part with its strong jaws. The mantid's lightning-quick reflexes and vice-like grip make it a powerful predator.

Sometimes the Asian giant hornet attacks alone. Other times it works in a group. Either way, the end result is often the death of its enemies. The hornet typically captures its prey in flight, using its super-strong mandibles. It practically never stings the prey it's hunting. The hornet usually bites instead. If a bite doesn't do the job, the hornet will sting repeatedly. The hornet's stings flood victims' bodies with deadly venom.

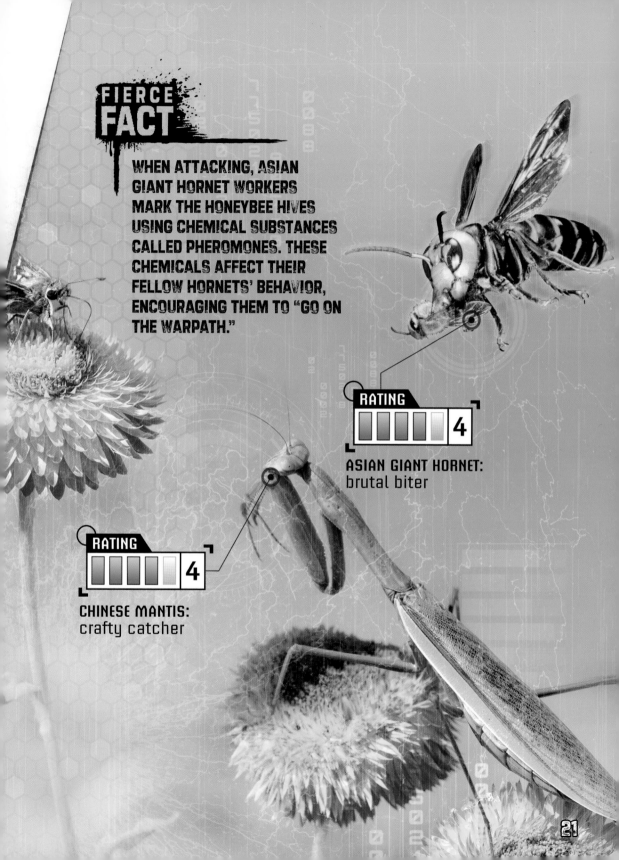

FIERCE FACT

WHEN ATTACKING, ASIAN GIANT HORNET WORKERS MARK THE HONEYBEE HIVES USING CHEMICAL SUBSTANCES CALLED PHEROMONES. THESE CHEMICALS AFFECT THEIR FELLOW HORNETS' BEHAVIOR, ENCOURAGING THEM TO "GO ON THE WARPATH."

RATING 4

ASIAN GIANT HORNET:
brutal biter

RATING 4

CHINESE MANTIS:
crafty catcher

Are you prepared for the big battle? Two mighty bugs are on the prowl. Each hopes to prove it's the toughest, most vicious insect in Asia.

In one corner is the lightning-quick, head-crunching Chinese mantis. He's spiky, large, and in charge. In the other corner is his opponent—the Asian giant hornet. Even his name strikes fear into the hearts of humans and other bugs. He's huge, relentless, and deadly. Nobody can say for certain which of these extra-enormous bugs will win the fight. But one thing is for sure—the winner is likely to be wounded along the way!

ONE LAST THING...

This fight is made up, just like in your favorite movies. These two bugs may occasionally fight in nature, but it's hard to say who would win. However, we know these bugs are ferocious fighters. So if you like a good bug battle, this should be a great show!

THE BATTLE BEGINS!

It's a sunny morning out in a flowery field. Birds twitter, crickets chirp, and leaves sway in the breeze. Yet this is the setting for what is to be a ferocious battle. Hiding in the tall grass, the Chinese mantis turns its triangular head back and forth. His huge eyes scan the scene. He's hungry. He waits patiently, his spiny forelegs raised and ready.

Suddenly, an Asian giant hornet buzzes by. In a brief stop, the hornet alights on a grassy patch near the mantis. In the blink of an eye, the mantis springs into action. He grabs the hornet with his barbed forelegs. He tries to bite the hornet with his sharp mandibles. But the hornet sends his stinger right through the mantis' exoskeleton. Ouch! The Chinese mantis retreats in pain, reeling from the nasty jab.

IN THE SUMMER OF 2013,
ASIAN GIANT HORNETS KILLED
40 PEOPLE AND INJURED
MORE THAN 1,600 IN CHINA'S
SHAANXI PROVINCE.

AMBUSH!

The mantis recovers. He holds his wings up to appear larger and scarier. His huge wings crackle. They sound like paper rubbing together. But the hornet is furious. His helicopter-like buzzing fills the space between the two enemies. The hornet zooms in to land on a bare patch of soil near the mantis.

Snap!

The mantis springs forward for Round Two, determined to make a kill. His front legs trap the hornet in a vice-like grip.

FIERCE FACT

MANTIDS COME IN MANY SHAPES AND SIZES. SOME LOOK LIKE FLOWERS. SOME LOOK LIKE LEAVES. SOME LOOK LIKE BLADES OF GRASS, STICKS, OR SPIKES. MANTIDS' ABILITY TO BLEND IN GIVES THEM A HUGE ADVANTAGE WHEN HIDING OR ATTACKING.

HEADS UP...
HEADS OFF!

With his stinger stuck facing away from the mantis, the hornet is at a disadvantage. The hornet tries one more time to sting his rival—but fails. In a matter of milliseconds, the mantis bites off the hornet's head. Chomp! The hornet's legs twitch briefly. Death comes quickly to the giant hornet.

The mantis leaves almost nothing of his giant meal. The hornet's wings flutter to the ground below. The Chinese mantis has devoured his opponent. Licking his chops, he removes any last guts from his front legs, antennae, and eyes. The Chinese mantis has taken out one of the fiercest insects in Asia!

GLOSSARY

carnivore (KAHR-nuh-vohr)—an animal that eats meat

compound eyes (KAHM-pound EYEZ)—eyes made up of many tiny lenses densely packed together

decapitate (di-KAP-uh-tate)—to cut off the head

exoskeleton (ek-soh-SKE-luh-tuhn)—a structure on the outside of an animal that gives it support

foreleg (FOHR-leg)—a front leg

mandible (MAN-duh-buhl)—strong mouthparts used for chewing

predator (PRED-uh-tur)—an animal that hunts other animals for food

prey (PRAY)—an animal hunted by another animal for food

species (SPEE-sheez)—a group of animals with similar features

thorax (THO-raks)—the middle of the three main divisions of an insect's body

toxic (TOK-sik)—poisonous

venom (VEN-um)—a liquid poison made by an animal to kill its prey

READ MORE

Bone, Emily. *The Usborne Book of Big Bugs*. London: Usborne Publishing, 2012.

Hesper, Sam. *Praying Mantises*. Animal Cannibals. New York: Powerkids Press, 2015.

Maley, Adrienne Houk. *20 Fun Facts About Praying Mantises*. New York: Gareth Stevens Publishing, 2013.

Terry, Paul. *Deadly Animals*. Top 10 for Kids. London: TickTock Books, 2015.

INTERNET SITES

FactHound offers a safe, fun way to find Internet sites related to this book. All of the sites on FactHound have been researched by our staff.

Here's all you do:

Visit *www.facthound.com*

Type in this code: 9781491480670

Check out projects, games and lots more at
www.capstonekids.com

INDEX